Published by Freddy Ocasio Publishing
December 18,2017

ISBN-13: 978-0692995921
ISBN-10: 0692995927

Library of Congress Control Number: 2017919244

Any people depicted in stock imagery provided by Thinkstock are models,
and such images are being used for illustrative purposes only.

Certain stock image © Thinkstock.

This book is printed in acid-free paper.

Because of the dynamic nature of the Internet, any web addresses or link
contained in this book may have changed since publication and may no longer be valid.

Liam's Life with Autism

Sensory Overload

FREDDY OCASIO

ILLUSTRATED BY

FREELY ABRIGO

Liam's Life with Autism, Sensory Overload is a story of a boy name Liam that has autism. Liam has been diagnosed with Sensory Processing Disorder ("SPD").

SPD can manifest itself in two different forms, hypersensitivity and hyposensitivity. Liam suffers with hypersensitivity, which means he has extreme sensitivity to noise, crowds, touch, texture, bright lights, certain clothing, and a change in routine.

The book allows you to see how SPD can interfere with an autistic child's daily function. Because the environment impacts Liam's life so profoundly, all situations can be full of stress and pain in Liam's everyday life.

Liam is like any other boy who enjoys playing with his favorite toy, dancing, or just being around the people he loves but because of his speech limitations, he cannot express his feelings, his wants or his needs.

When Liam is faced with the inability to express himself, he becomes frustrated and acts out inappropriately, which causes people to misunderstand Liam as being bad when, in fact, he's just mad.

This is Liam.
Liam is different in many ways.
He senses things in different ways.

The Five Senses For Children with Autism

Sense of Sight
I do not like the sun and other bright lights.

Sense of Taste
I am picky and do not like new foods and how they feel in my mouth.

Sense of Touch
I do not like tags in my clothing and I do not like to be tickled or hugged.

Sense of Hearing
I am overly sensitive to loud sounds and noises.

Sense of Smell
I am always smelling things like food, perfumes, and bad odor.

Liam and Sofia, sister and brother.
Rarely, do you see one without the other.

Sophia helps Liam with the things he can not yet do
Like buttoning his coat and tying his shoes.

Liam has autism and it's hard for him to interact with others.
Sometimes Liam wishes he could just hide under the covers.

At times when Liam's senses become overloaded.
He lets out a scream because he can not control it.

Liam's day is not easy at all.
This is what he goes through as I recall.

On the way to school Liam got mad.
He didn't like the smell of someone passing gas.

At breakfast what made Liam scrunch up his face,
was the cereals' color, texture, smell, and taste.

Liam did not like when his routine was changed because he does not like to see the schedule rearranged.

It's not that Liam is acting out or being bad,
he just does not know how to speak when he gets mad.

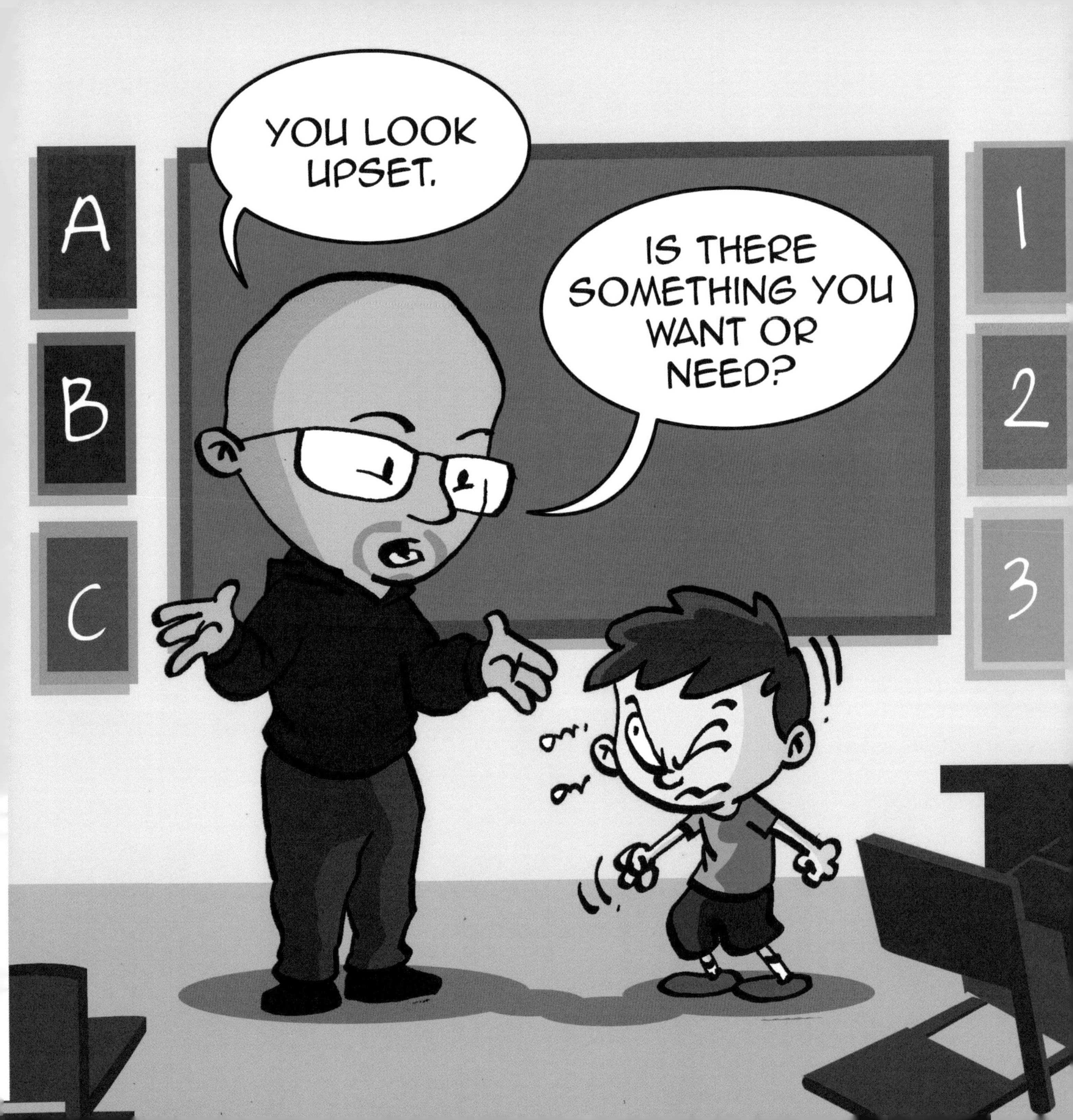
YOU LOOK UPSET.
IS THERE SOMETHING YOU WANT OR NEED?
A
B
C
1
2
3

Because of his balance at recess Liam got upset,
when he could not kick the ball into the net.

During class pictures the flash hurt Liam's eyes and made him want to cry, cry, cry.

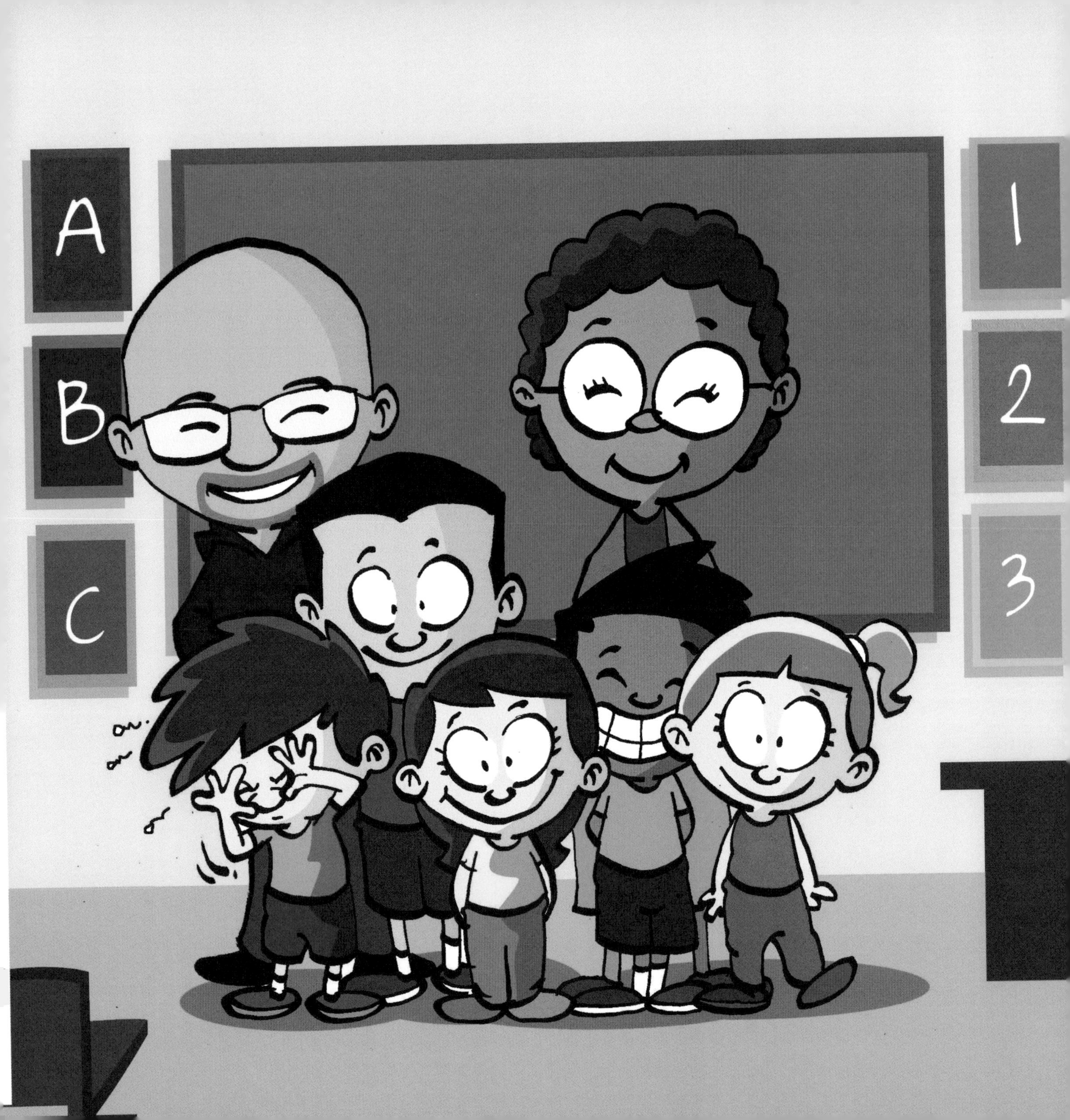
A
B
C
1
2
3

During math class the students were cheering.
But the loud sounds hurt Liam's hearing.

Liam had a party with all of his friends.
He drew a picture of them using a pen.

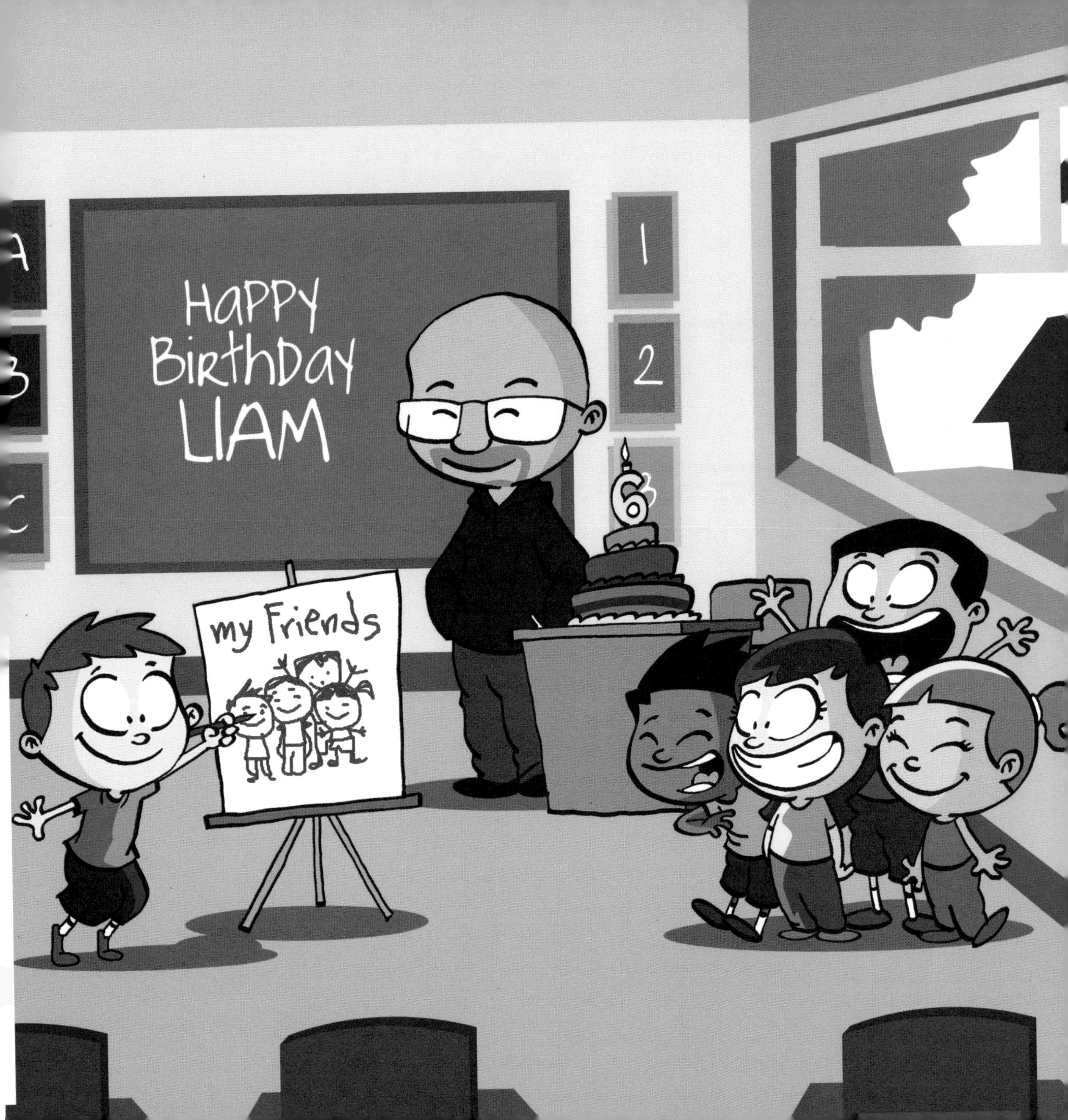

Happy
BirthDay
LIAM
my Friends

When the music was not so loud
Liam danced every time he got a chance.

When Liam got home the tag on his shirt was touching his skin, luckily Sofia was there to tuck it in.

Liam loves to be at home where there is no noise and he can just play with his favorite toy.

Liam is like you and me in many ways,
once you get to know him you will be amazed.

HOW I HELP MY BROTHER LIAM

I LOVE MY BROTHER LIAM. WHEN HE EXPERIENCES SENSORY PROCESSING DISORDER (SPD) BECAUSE OF A SMELL, SOUND, TASTE, TOUCH OR SIGHT, IT CAN BE TOO MUCH FOR HIM TO DEAL WITH. THESE ARE SOME THINGS THAT WORK WELL FOR ME TO MANAGE THESE SITUATIONS.

SIGHT

WHEN THE LIGHT BOTHERS LIAM, I USE A LAMP INSTEAD OF FLUORESCENT LIGHTING AND I USE BLACKOUT CURTAINS TO MINIMIZE LIGHT AND OR SUNGLASSES.

HEARING

I GIVE LIAM HEADPHONES OR EARPLUGS WHEN THERE IS A LOT OF NOISE. ASKING YES OR NO QUESTIONS ARE EASIER TO RESPOND TO, AND CAN BE ANSWERED WITH THUMBS UP/THUMBS DOWN.

TOUCH

I LET LIAM KNOW WHEN I AM GOING TO HUG HIM BY ASKING HIM, "MAY I HUG YOU LIAM? CLOTHING TAGS SHOULD BE FIXED OR REMOVED SO THAT IT DOES NOT BOTHER HIM.

SMELL

I TRY TO REMOVE AS MANY UNPLEASANT SCENTS AS POSSIBLE FROM AROUND LIAM. THE SCENT OF PERFUMES, SCENTED DETERGENTS, AIR FRESHENERS, SCENTED CANDLES, SCENTED LOTIONS, HAIRSPRAY, THE SMELL OF FOOD AND OTHER SMELLS AND SCENTS CAN TRIGGER A NERVOUS RESPONSE.

TASTE

I ALLOW LIAM TO EXPLORE HIS FOOD WITH HIS HANDS SO HE CAN GET USE TO THE TEXTURES BEFORE HE PUTS IT IN HIS MOUTH. I GIVE LIAM DIFFERENT FORMS OF FOOD USING TRIAL AND ERROR AND I ONLY DO ONE FOOD AT A TIME TO FIND OUT WHAT HE LIKES. WHILE EATING I WOULD HAVE LIAM LISTEN TO MUSIC, PLAY WITH A TOY, OR I WOULD READ A BOOK TO HELP TAKE ATTENTION AWAY FROM EATING.

DISCLAIMER: EVERY INDIVIDUAL, WHETHER A CHILD OR AN ADULT, EXPERIENCES DIFFERENT LEVELS OF SENSORY INPUT THAT CAN CAUSE A SENSORY OVERLOAD. CHILDREN WITH SPD AND/OR AUTISM SPECTRUM DISORDER CAN HAVE A DIFFICULT TIME SELF-REGULATING. THEREFORE, PARENTS, TEACHERS AND CAREGIVERS SHOULD RECOGNIZE THE VARIOUS TRIGGERS. PLEASE SPEAK WITH A PROFESSIONAL, READ BOOKS ON THE SUBJECT MATTER AND DO RESEARCH TO LEARN HOW TO APPROPRIATELY DEAL WITH THESE SITUATIONS.

FREDDY OCASIO was born and raised in The Bronx, he is married with three children and continues to live and work in New York.

Growing up with Speech, Language Disorders and ADHD (Attention Deficit Hyperactivity Disorder), Freddy experienced first-hand how it felt not to fit in because he was different from others. Early on in his life he was placed in Special Education classes but hard work and perseverance quickly earned him placement among the general education classes within the New York City public school system. He graduated from Medgar Evers College with an Associates, he subsequently received a Bachelors in Speech and Audiology from Lehman College and went on to graduate with a Master's in Education from Mercy College.

Freddy's goal in life is to make a difference in the lives of children with disabilities, having experienced good and bad times because of his behavior and limited speech. He went on to work with students with multiple disabilities then the emotionally disturbed population but his true love is working with children who have autism, which he has done for many years to this day.

Presently, he has put his considerable teaching skills and vast knowledge into writing his first book, Liam's Life with Autism, Sensory Overload. Freddy's desire is that this book will bring more awareness to a wider audience. Children and adults reading his book will have a greater understanding of the characteristics of Autism and what it feels like to live with Sensory Processing Disorders. He plans to follow it up with many more titles in the future.

Freddy's favorite quote comes from the American journalist, Jim Watkins, which thoroughly depicts his life long journey. "A river cuts through rock, not because of its power, but because of its persistence."

Printed in Great Britain
by Amazon